For Gabrielle and Achille

Thanks to Josette Grandazzi, Catherine Marquet, Hugues Charreyron and Annick Duboscq

In the same collection
My Little Pompidou Centre
My Little Cluny
My Little Louvre
My Little Orsay
My Little Picasso
My Little Quai Branly
My Little Versailles

Translation: Isabel Ollivier
Photographics: Hanna Nelson
Design and layout: Chloé du Colombier
Photoengraving: I.G.S.
Printed by Mame, Tours

© Adagp, 2010
© Succession Picasso, 2010
© Succession H. Matisse, 2010
© 2010 – Réunion des musées nationaux
   49, rue Étienne-Marcel
   75001 Paris

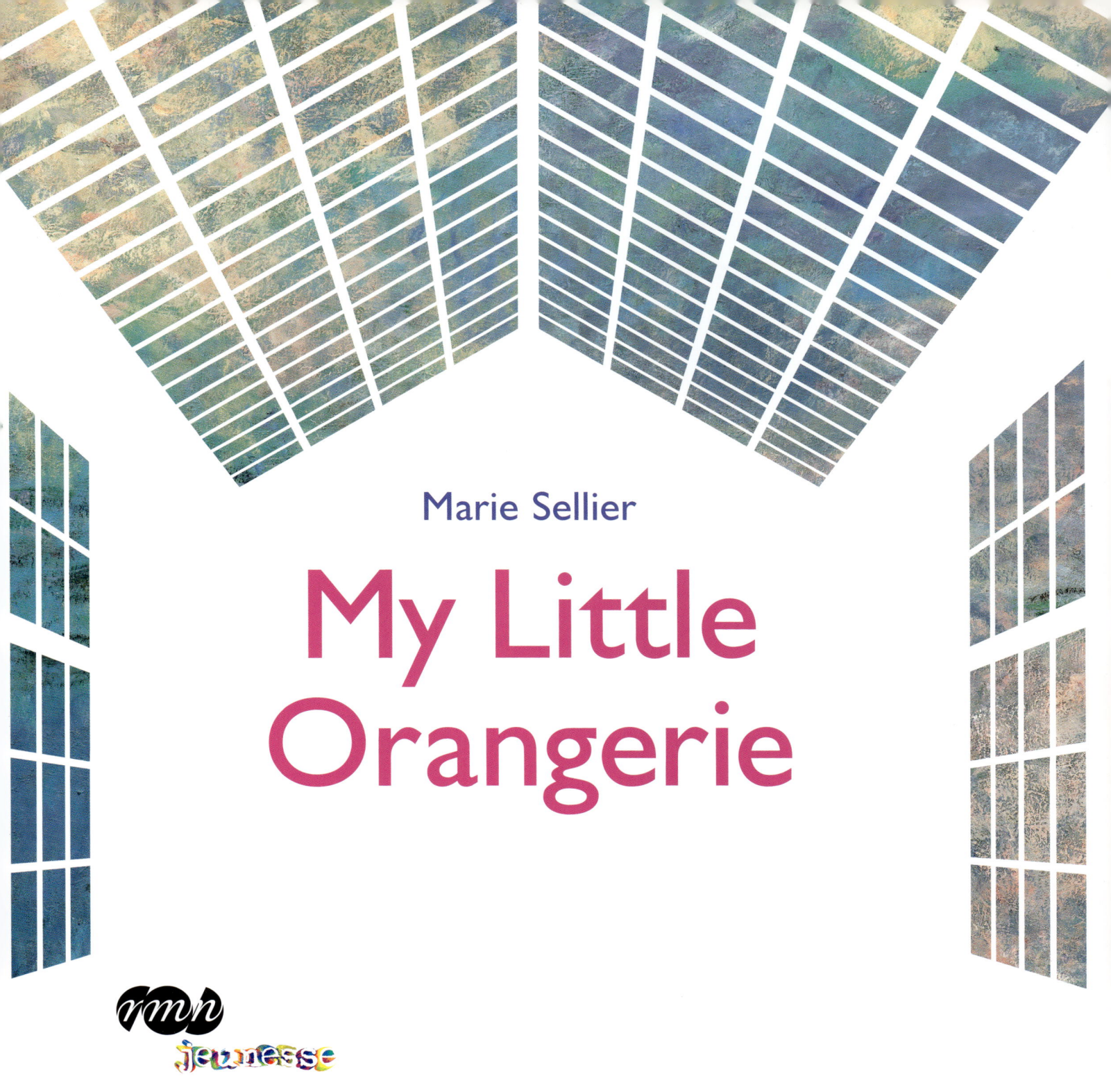

Long, long ago, before cars, telephones and electric lights,
when gentlemen wore top hats and ladies wore huge crinolines,
an avenue in the Tuileries garden in Paris was lined with orange trees
in big square boxes. In winter, they were taken inside the Orangerie
to protect them from the frost until the following spring.

Now the orange trees have gone so they do not need the pretty glassed building in the winter. But other fruit and flowers have taken their place. Claude Monet filled the Orangerie with his fabulous water garden and paintings but there was still room for the paintings collected by Paul Guillaume and Jean Walter.

there is ... a morning

A new day on earth, a new morning.

Scarcely a ripple on the big pond

under a clear blue sky. The air is transparent.

The old painter gazes at his marvellous garden on the water.

The water lilies on their bright green raft of leaves

have not yet opened their big rosy petals.

All is calm. Birdsong, a faint scratching.

The scratching comes from the artist's brush

going back and forth on a huge rough canvas.

On his palette, pinks mix with blues,

mauves, straw yellow with a tinge of green.

Slowly, taking his time,

Claude Monet paints the sky mirrored in the water.

Claude Monet
Water Lilies: Morning
Circa 1914-1926

there is ... Paul posing

This boy is called Paul, like his father.

Paul-the-son and Paul-the-painter. Paul Cézanne.

Paul has just come in from school.

He's still wearing his navy blue smock.

At school he ran around in the courtyard with his friends,

but now, he is sitting askew on the wing chair as still as a statue.

His father gets cross if he moves when he is posing.

His father is rather stern. Everyone knows that.

Paul stares straight ahead. Hard to know what he is thinking of.

Nothing perhaps. At least, he says nothing.

Paul-the-painter puts little dabs of blue on his son's cheek.

For the shadow. And a smear of red on his lips,

like a girl.

Paul Cézanne
Portrait of the Artist's Son
1881-188

there is ... Coco playing

Another son, another father.

Renoir doesn't make Coco pose,

he just watches him playing.

And while his little boy is playing, he paints him.

A touch of blue: "Hands up!" shouts the sergeant on the hill.

A touch of white: "Saved!" cries the Indians' prisoner.

A touch of brown: "Let's run! Let's hide behind a tree!" says the Indian chief.

A touch of green: "Too late," groans the Indian brave.

A touch of black: "We're done for!" they both murmur.

"We've won!" shouts Coco.

"Well done, my boy!" Renoir claps his hands.

Auguste Renoir
Claude Renoir playing
1905

there is ... a cartload of people

"Gee up, Rosa!" calls Mr Junier, the man with the curly moustache and a middle parting. But Rosa doesn't budge.

"We are not going to sit here all afternoon!" grumbles Mrs Junier, the lady with the grey bun.

"As stubborn as a mule!" pipes up her niece Lea.

"Yap, yap" barks the queer little dog on her lap.

"Please, Rosa, be a love!" begs the little girl with a grown-up face. But Rosa does not budge.

Five people and a dog is far too heavy a load to pull.

And with these blinkers on, she can't see the view.

Rose wants to be free, like the dogs beside her.

And what does Mr Rousseau in his straw hat think of it all?

He thinks: "Never mind the ride, they'll make lovely picture."

Henri Rousseau (Le Douanier)
Mr Junier's Carriage
1908

there are... houses doing gym

One, two, three, all together now,

a step to the right, a step to the left,

swing over and back.

Open the windows wide,

puff out your chests,

breathe in by the door,

sway your hips,

bend your roofs to the left

and stretch, stretch right up to the sky.

Taller, taller,

hands on hips, and down again.

Breathe in.

One, two, three, and we start again...

Chaïm Soutine
The Houses
Circa 1920-1921

there is ... a garden on the water

The old painter is mad about flowers.

He is a wonderful artist,

but he is a grand gardener, too.

He has filled his big garden at Giverny

with peonies and irises,

roses, dahlias and lilies.

And water lilies float like riverboats

on his great pond.

In the shade of reeds and kalmias

lie patches of lily leaves

with tatters of blue sky between them.

Claude Monet
Water Lilies: Morning
Circa 1914-1926

there is ... a garden at the world's end

Down here on the island of Hiva Oa,

there is a garden of Eden,

where silvery trees,

coconut palms and bananas grow.

The sea is never far away.

A painter made his home here,

a man called Paul Gauguin.

Children are coming through the high grass

to see him. A grown-up is with them.

They're coming to see the man who makes men and trees,

a white medicine man who copies the world in his own way

with a stick and bright colours.

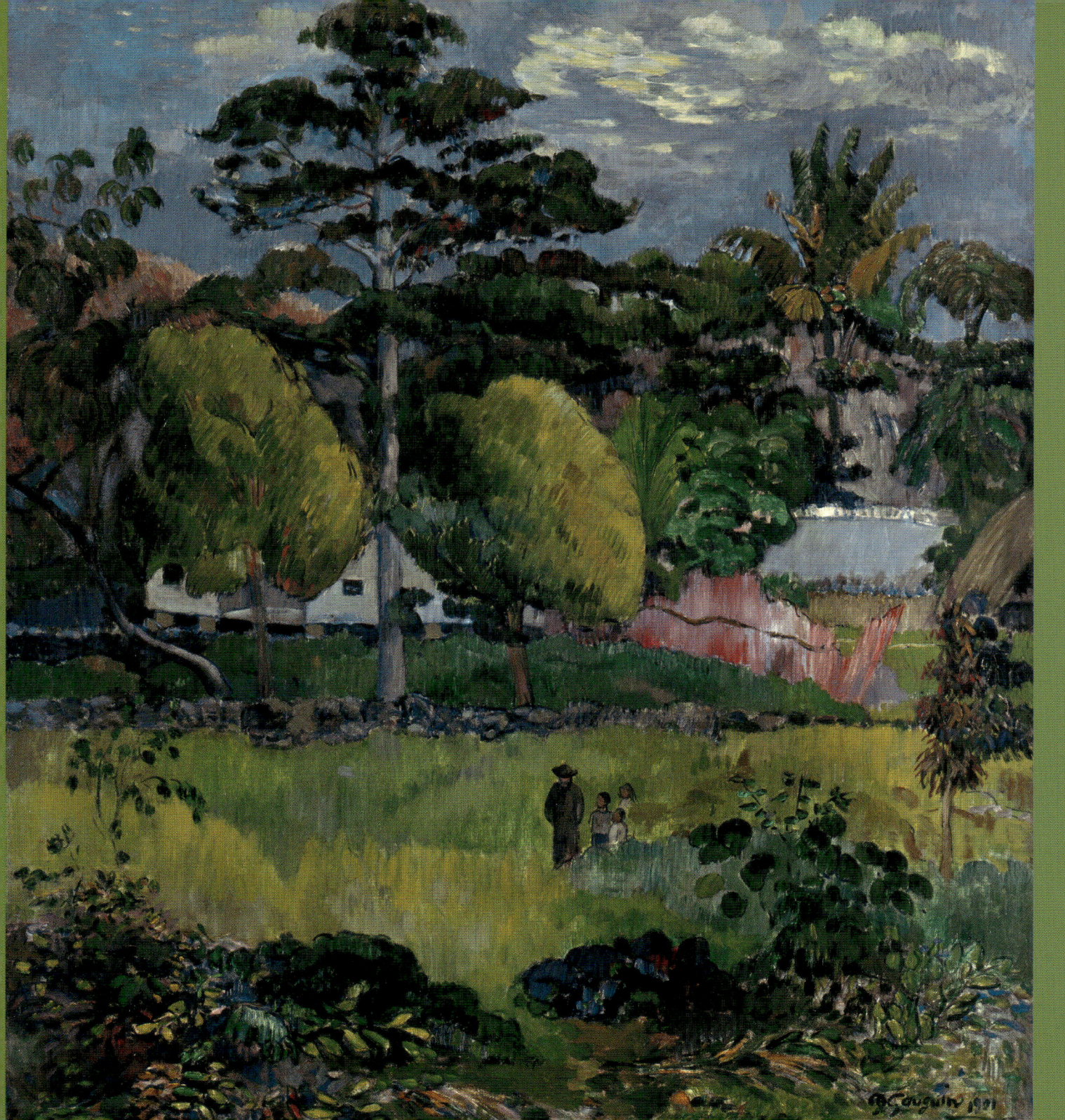

there are... apples

Yellow apples, red apples,

autumn apples,

and two little biscuits on a blue plate.

Scrumptious apples,

eating apples and cooking apples.

Have a biscuit, I'll have the other one.

We'll leave the apples for Cezanne

because he paints them better than anyone.

Paul Cézanne
Apples and Biscuits
Circa 1880

there is... a sleeping table

"Wake up, wake up!" calls the salad basket

hopping up and down on the plates.

"It's time to make the meal and set the table.

Frying pan, you cook the onions.

Grill, you do the meat.

We'll put the lettuce in the soup tureen,

the rice in the colander. Come on, quickly!

Grate the cheese and chop the parsley. Hurry up, scissors!

Corkscrew, you go and get the bottle.

Someone fill the carafe with water.

Oh, there's no glass! Go and get a glass!

Good heavens! They are all asleep in this still life! Still dead more like!

You'd think we were in Sleeping Beauty's kitchen."

André Derain
The Kitchen Table
Circa 1922

there is... a talking tray

"I wouldn't mind a drop to drink,"

says Picasso's glass, wiggling its stem.

He has an awfully sharp nose.

"Pay your bill first,

and then we'll see,"

says the stout bottle lady

tying a white apron around her big tummy.

That makes the fruit bowl cackle over his paper hens.

The table keeps its drawer tight shut

and nearly rocks its top off.

But it is all bluff.

Everybody knows that the bottle boss

never says no to the wine glass.

Pablo Picasso
Large Still Life
1917

there is... a traveller's apprentice

Modigliani's young apprentice

has eyes snipped from the Norman sky,

hair made from autumn leaves

and skin as golden as the paths of Provence.

His shirt has been cut from grey Paris walls,

his waistcoat and jacket are Brittany slate,

his trousers a murky river after rain.

And he is dreaming he is a bird

soaring above a pretty world.

Leaving masonry and carpentry far behind.

What would it matter?

He is a dreamer's apprentice, a traveller's apprentice,

bewitched and bewitching.

Amedeo Modigliani
The Young Apprentice
1918-1919

there are ... two girls waiting

In a bedroom by the sea,

two girls are waiting in the pale light

of a winter's day. Or spring perhaps.

The washed out colours of passing time:

faded sky blues, pearl greys, porcelain whites,

soft mauves, dull reds, blond and tarnished gold.

Soon the anemones will drop their petals.

Outside stands a single, spiky palm.

Who are they waiting for?

What are they waiting for?

For the artist to finish his picture perhaps?

When Matisse lays down his brushes,

they will go for a walk on the sand.

Henri Matisse
The Boudoir
1921

there are ... clouds on the water

A few bright white clouds

scudding over the water.

The old painter does not need to lift his head

to see them racing over the sky.

The lily pond mirrors

whatever goes on up there.

With the tip of his brush, the old man

whips his whites to a froth, as light as air,

and makes the clouds whirl

over the turquoise and azure

of the big pond at Giverny.

Each day, Claude Monet reinvents his lily pond

on the huge panels stuck on the wall.

Claude Monet
Water Lilies: Clouds
Circa 1914-1926

there is... a secret

What is she whispering?

You can steal closer

and prick up your ears

but it is no use, the secret is well kept.

We will never know why the little girl's cheek is so red

or why the big girl looks so dreamy.

All we have is a portrait of two girls

in old fashioned dresses,

one wearing a straw hat, the other a ribbon.

Red hair, brown hair,

two pretty faces, snub noses

and round cheeks.

Two good little girls.

And that is all we will ever know.

Auguste Renoir
Portrait of Two Girls
1890-1892

there is ... no smile

What a grumpy face!

A little girl in a red frock

whose legs are sinking

into a grass carpet dotted with poppies

and black and white daisies!

Her doll is grumpy too!

Not a ghost of a smile!

Don't think that playing means having fun.

Grown-ups never understand anything!

"Go away. Leave us alone.

Raymonde and I hate being watched!"

Henri Rousseau (Le Douanier)
Child with a Doll
Circa 1892?
Circa 1904-1905

there is... a scribbled-on portrait

Look at the top of the picture, on the left.

Thirteen letters: PAUL GUILLAUME. Like two first names.

The name of this man with his felt hat, natty moustache

and tightly tied tie. A man with sloping shoulders,

smoking as he gazes at us.

"Yes, that's me. Paul Guillaume."

He is friendly with lots of artists. And he is also an art dealer.

He likes the work of Amedeo Modigliani, who painted his portrait.

He has flair. Modigliani calls him NOVO PILOTA,

which is Italian for "new pilot".

Yes, Paul Guillaume is the new pilot of the art world,

a sort of talent scout. He was the man who collected

the paintings now in the Orangerie.

Amedeo Modigliani
Paul Guillaume, Novo Pilota
1915

there is... a little ship

Rain in the funnels, awash to the gunnels.

Red-white-blue on a blue-black sea.

Vive la France!

Lowering skies, oooh!

Towering waves, nooo!

Lightning flashes, wow!

Thunder crashes, pow!

Man overboard! Oh Lord!

Sailors in the drink. We'll sink!

Skipper's on the deck, oh heck!

It's Captain Rousseau, uh-oh!

He's no landlubber...

His oil paint won't wash off, by gosh!

So his ship rides the waves and we're saved!

Henri Rousseau (Le Douanier)
Ship in a Storm
Circa 1899

there is... an evening

The end of a day.

The sun has lit a fire in the sky

and thrown a cloak of pink and gold

over the lily pond, a precious evening cloak

embroidered with blue grasses.

The fire will not last long,

a few minutes, no more.

But the old painter would not miss the evening glow

for anything in the world.

All day long he has painted, scraped, repainted

the great panel of his waterborne dream.

This evening, he is pleased with it.

Now it is time to leave the studio.

Good night, Mr Monet.

Claude Monet
Water Lilies: Sunset
Circa 1914-1922

You will find
the two girls waiting,
the garden on the water and the little ship
and all the others in the **Orangerie** in **Paris**.
Open every day except Tuesdays.
www.musee-orangerie.fr

Cover and endpapers:
Claude Monet, *Water Lilies: Morning,* Circa 1914-1926 (detail)
Henri Rousseau (Le Douanier), *Mr Junier's Carriage,* 1908 (details)

Pages 5, 6-7, 44:
Claude Monet, *Water Lilies: Clouds,* Circa 1914-1926 (details)

Photo credits:
Réunion des musées nationaux
© F. Raux: p. 11, 13, 15, 23, 35, 37, 41
© H. Lewandowski: p. 9, 17, 19, 21, 25, 27, 29, 33, 39, 43
© T. Le Mage: p. 31

Law no. 49 956 of 16 July 1949
on children's books

Registered: April 2010
ISBN 978-2-7118-5742-5
JC 70 5742